UNDERWOOD LOG

Underwood Log

by

W. H. New

OOLICHAN BOOKS
LANTZVILLE, BRITISH COLUMBIA, CANADA
2004

National Library of Canada Cataloguing in Publication

New, W. H. (William Herbert), 1938-
         Underwood log / W.H. New.

Poem.

ISBN 0-88982-193-3

         I. Title.

PS8577.E776U54 2004   C811'.54   C2004-901003-4

The Canada Council | Le Conseil des Arts
for the Arts | du Canada

We gratefully acknowledge the support of the Canada Council for the Arts for our publishing program.

BRITISH
COLUMBIA
ARTS COUNCIL

Grateful acknowledgement is also made to the BC Ministry of Tourism, Small Business and Culture for their financial support.

We acknowledge the financial support of the Government of Canada through the Book Publishing Industry Development Program for our publishing activities.

Published by
Oolichan Books
P.O. Box 10, Lantzville
British Columbia, Canada
V0R 2H0
Printed in Canada

this book is for Peggy,
for Frances and Richie, Paddy, Hap,
and friends of a lifetime, around the world:

even in the forest
no-one writes alone:

A forest is language; accumulated years.

—Murray Bail, *Eucalyptus*

Our grammar might teach us to divide the world into active subjects and passive objects, but in a coevolutionary relationship every subject is also an object, every object a subject. That's why it makes just as much sense to think of agriculture as something the grasses did to people as a way to conquer the trees.

—Michael Pollan, *The Botany of Desire*

names of elsewhere
take you travelling:

you tell your story travelling, trailing
others, those who live, and those who have lived, re-locating:
some were here before you, thinking themselves in place,
some will come after,
bones and bones, an underwood of dreaming

home now, and now later,
trees around us, paradox and
past, yes, the living going on, desire
at the ready—
or is it expectation, blind,
sun at some meridian, and shadowlines
cross-
hatching into time:

take place, for instance,
neighbourhood—

plant your feet at the local crossroads,
what do you see there? frost and tangled
tropic? pall-grey rain?
what words hang stammering
in the accident of air, and leave you
here, as near as memory,
syllables as tumbling as green?

only Away:

for only by going away, gambling your life
into the halting underwood,
can you or I,
chilled and welcome, once
again
return—

think of those you read about, those
antique saints and halting scholars, wrestling

angels into alphabets, minuscules and
gleaming sins in rows—

chase them if you dare, down
animal tracks and city alleyways,

random as seed: they'll lead you into
storybook and wild mind, overseas and

inland—nothing will shade you from
ghost and glare except your willingness

to hear—you might think you're in command,
counting your way by milepost and mask,

but listen: what do you say,
and what do you apprehend—

      tree
      shrub

      grass
      root

      canopy
      understory

you have a name for everything
      oh?

August '02, and news on the internet announces
someone's broken four fingers and thumb off

Mary MacKillop's right hand—*Shocking*, says
Father Don—and that's the story:

if pressed, the web will add a bit more, starting with
Sister Mary's cantankerous gripes against

direction (she'd work
outside the rules if need be—

and need *was*—and so the slow path to
sainthood):

you can see her lifesize statue, too,
carved from a single trunk of

camphorwood, there in St. Stephen's
Queensland, where

severed fingers lie on the floor—
you see them: though the web can't spin

the intensity of scent, or candlewax,
or reason:

shocking, says Father Don, assuming
vandals where she's now revered:

what if history finds a penitent instead,
desperate for miracles, who reaches

please, hold my hand,
squeezes, feels sculpted wooden bones

begin to disengage,
and flees Stephen

empty,
reversing into stones:

think of Joan, in Old Orléans, clutching her stake
while fire eats at her thumbs

and seven fingers: crying out the king's name,
spider, electric, blue—

(travelling to find the story, naming
points instead, co-ordinates of moment,

you pitch yourself in space, think
tap root and oak, while under-

ground, rhizomes are hustling al-
ready into tomorrow, days ahead and

different hemispheres—now is past:
someone's writing you out of the

ordinary, canting crosses and
nautical lines:

look around: who
else do you see?

maybe it's you shaking
silence into lines)—

listen: a thick Louisiana night recites
crickets under house-high magnolia cones—

  a man imitating Twain tells the tale of the
  celebrated frog—another man's reminded

of trained grasshoppers in Viet Nam,
before the Action started, racing

  (though whether to claim the past
  or praise its passing is less clear)—

the St. Charles tram rattles by on schedule
out towards Anne Rice and plantation country,

  leaving the tomb of the Voodoo Queen
  back in the Quarter, where a single sax on a

3rd-floor wrought iron gallery worries pain into impro-
visation, brackish and drifting, bodies recom-

  bining in heat and leveed love:
  a civil war is still going on, the scent of

plumbago and rutting decay: living here
testifies to bay and Mississippi, players dealing

  menace, the unforeseen, magnolia stories told
  out of order, real slow—

so when you're drawn back into the
sheer

puffery that candypinks a
wet city April (PR

plumblossom stuffing the malls,
glossy postcards enamelling the

super
natural),

you're only just beginning to see,
under the gauze, days

extend, spring
                action—

where is here?
Kitsilano: Kitsilano's edge

a place of trees?
a grid of cross-streets: larch, balsam,
arbutus, yew,
the avenues are numbered

and this is where you live?
in the intervals, along the margins

you call it home?
why do you ask?

say I:

say *forest* and who ever thinks of the
scarlet bottlebrush (armies of banksia men

storming the nation's bedroom walls?)—
and what if they do:
                    the manchineel spitting

        poison in the axeman's eyes, the giant kauri
        heaving out of the earth the wrong way,

        crushing by intent some johnny-come-lately
        beanstalk-clambering fly?—
                            who's to say

the bottlebrush won't stir unrest as well,
unfold suddenly into what's unknown—

the storybooks—*Oz, Hansel & Gretel*—
gnarl treetrunks into monsters, limbs into

traps: branches
shut like mouths behind wandering children,

swallow them whole
(and somehow the children are always to blame,

stepping out of line, inviting the trees to
eat them)—

      you know the tamarind, the
      hanging tree,

      will have them in the end—
      if you believe the tale:

though tellers don't always
tell you:

ordinary ogres
claim to own the young,

tell tales,
and threaten them with trees—

ombú: you know it but do not believe it, the
sponge tree of Argentina, so wet it

will not burn, though it cuts like lard:
imagine it with Darwin, his eyes cataloguing

difference, evaluating fit—what
language did he hear?

did he poke at the syllables
and hear *om* (holiness)?

or negative *bū* (holiness denied)?
ombros, perhaps, Greek rain, or

shortened *o mega*, the great *o*, *alpha*-less,
nothing at the core but poison?

border-crossing became a habit,
if never familiar,

but who could brace for what he'd
find (absorption in the

nearest element, each understanding
a challenge to pattern)—

whatever does not accord:
exception or rule? is the

specimen odd or the tailored
circumnavigator

who measures in advance
the great ocean?

did Charles take an axe to the
ombú, say, and

test his resistance?
did he ever think of the Omaha?

　　(Sioux:
　　those who travel upstream)—

or read in Timothy Taylor's book, about
one man standing

fixed on a single moment,
knowing motion (*the infinite coordinates*

of an intimate landscape,
sweeping away in all directions)

and knowing this:
whoever is always moving is

never here
or there:

so what is the point (*neither-*
here-nor-there?)—

only despots and fear
pronounce irrelevance:

you seek alternatives,
a place to plant the feet:

Stromovka, Stanley Park,
the place of trees—

risky business, this: this
yen for counter-demonstration,

a place to lose north—
so how, without compass,

do you tell a single moment
into space—

dendroid: (1) like a tree in form, dendritic,
(2) a *dendrite*, the nerves branching fine,

finer, down every bodyway: we live
tree, hear *tree*, talk and walk and touch

tree, dendroids in
urban forest—

in the foothills of the Himalayas
rhododendrons grow wild, head high and

higher, rose-madder roaming the
canopy: imagine them human,

wild men springing mind into light,
thinking *tree*—

from outside, you can catalogue a tree:
        count the parts,

leaf, bark, slick layer, wood, drum
        forest into Tom-Thomson wild—

or analyze it:
        apical meristem, or *lateral,*

the cell divisions rooting and shooting, or
        (later) adding girth:

the analyst's eyes devise pattern, mutter
        parallels—or else declare

thing, difference—
        (words like *xylem* and *phloem*

distribute water and food,
        the *periderm* covers the

phalloderm, outer protecting inner,
        cork ringing the

vascular system):
        at the end of it all,

photosynthesis: transformation
        still a puzzle—

from inside:
is there a view from inside?

(splitting cell and birth pangs, that
first gasp of air, the necessary

lunging after food, water,
separate space?)

saplings grow fibre, adding the
bark later, to keep from being

seen, vulnerable:
(repairing wounds awkwardly,

knowing the trickiness of
branching out, dreaming

strength—perhaps size, power,
though maybe never words like *vascular*

and *phellem*): how the inside
shapes the world

(though find a world that
doesn't think it shapes itself):

even the plain words will not do:
      red stem and *2x4*—

they claim the precedence of sight, the
      numberlog of system:

it's at the edge where cells go on
      deliberating space,

inside where they speak in riddles,
      tongues of reach and reading—

what is your name, Charles Borromeo?
did you ever answer Medici on your mother's side,

favourite of Pius the Fourth, bishop, benefactor,
Palestrina's patron—or just say

Charles, generous to the plague-ridden poor?
did you guess you'd show up later

in an Oxford Book of Saints
on the page next to Borgia, your countryman

(the one who preached fine lines:
Ignatius trained you both)—

and did you ever think *Saint?*
(do the good regret thinking *That was good?*)

What is your name?
            N or M.—

you made your name (yes,
that's what people say, you

made your name, reading
signs and rhythm in stars and figures and leaves)

as a bureaucrat—did you ever say that?—
designing catechisms:

> *What is your name, who made you,*
> *what is your first responsibility?*

the stories they tell of you (lisp and lavish enter-
tainments, lingering trips to the Bernese Alps)

hint
at how you pulled those renegades

back from Calvin, parried
silvertongued sorcerors,

railed against the witches flying
west among the Swiss and sinister pines and

Zwingli:
did you also look for vampires there,

or did they wait for centuries more, howling
nightly in numberless stars

for mirrors and stokers and Anne?
names: streetcars into the leaching night:

who is *N*? who is *M*?
          where is *I*?

what do you see at the bay window
that opens onto Larch Street?
lintel, pane, blind, reflection

who do you see there?
I in shadow, trunk and limbs,
superimposition on a
single twisted spruce

and neighbourhood is near, Kitsilano?
ash and axes, August in the afternoon

do you figure in the season, stir
possibility and blossom?
eye, watching the wind:
maple parachutes spin
casings at the curb

a bluejay ratchets in the apple tree,
peremptory as Heston on the rock, rasping

pharaoh's chariots into
red oblivion: *attention:*

> *ignore the finches,*
> *stone the crows,*

eye cocked undertuft on seed, shadow,
camera:

> the blue
> snaps watchers out of drift:

manganese, cyan, colour its own
wrench and weapon, sinuate in the

charred grey:
> *follow me, follow*

me—where: *'some charley*
inviting the storm'—

> in behind the screen the puppets
> file into wooden motion:

they do not draw the string
that dances them—

call yourself what you will, say
Henry, Terry, Sam,

the names don't matter: you have
many, and not out of the woods yet:

Henry's the blind one, Terry afraid,
Sam'll do anything (who do you

hear
stalking the undergrowth, animate and

echo?)—*there's dead people here,*
says one,

and dead to come;
another carries moulded maple

sugar in a backpack;
neither knows how to predict the

third, maybe it's you,
lost among the ghost trunks,

rummaging for elephants,
abandoned graves—

you walk daily into the forest: trees
enclose you,

you do not notice,
lost in birling metaphor,

that eagles coursing overhead will

stop in the moment's air: you
haul the witch's cabin with you,

axes under your arm, listen for
manitou, the grey wolf howling

soon
while one by one the trees are disappearing—

you pack bandaids in case of a
minotaur, no matter the weather, he's

never there:
nor does he follow—

bread crumbs would serve as well—
and finches,

ever eagles' prey,
come to meet your hand—

imagine those others, wandering the
Appalachian hills, the mountainous Northwest,

attaching their names to trees: David Douglas
fir, tupelo Mark Gatesby, John

Tradescant (of *tradescantia*), and
Vancouver's man Archie Menzies (say it

Mingus, and watch
how he stands, recording

gymnosperms in his shiny hornbook): imagine
John Bartram, who called into being

the Franklin tree—*camellia-like*,
the garden guidebooks say,

American, once part of the understory, adding
now extinct in the wild—

did John B. ever think of this, and folksingers
vocalize the end? did the wandering

botanists ever meet up in a gaudy
singalong, *Black is the color*,

Green grow the rushes? imagine them
all in the same room—

gathered, say, by a
Franklin stove at the end of a long tramp,

drawing up to the burning logs
to keep the day's taxonomies dry—

what stories do they tell—
rumours at court, inventions,

freehold claims and clearings (post-it notes on
all the trees)—

and what do they leave out, besides
plotlines and barbed wire,

the war against the wildwood and
closing time—

face it:
as soon as a forest gets a name,

Sherwood, say, it stops being
wilderness: you go there, it's

full of the story-people, Bo-
peep and the dragon, with

stout heart and full quiver to
drive the point home, Transylvania:

the names always box you up,
equate the dark pines with witches,

the other side (they always say
the other side):

whoever the dauntless hero is, he
just possesses castle keeps and

green fields, which maybe accounts
for why a seance appeals: that

wrapped and slatted need to know for sure
if—

puzzling, this:
Bo was always keen to lose,

the dragon just to play with fire
(you've heard of Alexandria):

how they got stuck in the wood
is two stories, really,

theirs and the
head librarian's version, authorized:

though generally you get to hear
only the one—

for JH

take "The Cycads," for instance,
Judith Wright's brief meditation on the

    difficult antique:
    stone generations staring

    absence in the face, memory's
    loss, the puzzlement of sleep—

take the complicated
forests of ordinary things,

    birds, notebooks, cotton
    pillow cases,

    when to eat and when to
    suffocate (the weight of paper matches):

everything is darkness,
or might be darkness, forgery

    (the difference from light's unclear,
    sequencing awry)—

    except for the leaves:
    they flicker, unable to die,

    the body refusing,
    like sleep,

    like writing,
    to let go:

you prune memory instead, whittle a
syllable, lop a word away, open thickets

ruthlessly, and burn—
writing is

     overgrowing,
     peeling down to undershirt and image:

     the carver chipping idly at old wood,
     the arborist among the Gravensteins

     binding new stock onto standing roots,
     the old poet reading:

catch them in the bony moment they
make the first graft, glimpse

     Holofernes in the shadows,
     cycads in flame—

after a fire they're the
first to grow,

mini-lodgepoles, aspen, alder—and they
crowd mad-Boxing-Day for bargain air and

food, shootingup saplings, all
sugarhigh and limbs—

> why do you look past them at
> black and black, digital

> boneyards,
> fasten on the burn and

> do not see the bleeding over there, where
> weed flames in mimicry—

you can walk now without
breaking the crust:

why do you still need to
ask yourself permission,

why parcel the land in
shouting match and tremble—

> *mulga. bloodwood. gidgi.*
> (Thea Astley writes) *The stayers.*

> *The ones that keep cropping up*
> *after fire, after felling—*

but will I, she asks
(or the one who tells her tale)—

think about that:
who told? (don't tell)—

for on the dark days
you can still hear them,

chanting what they think is
solidarity:

> *sapwood sapwood*
> *heartwood fig*
>
> *tea-tree coffee-tree*
> *sugarcane pig*
>
> *you pick the coffeebean*
> *you pick the tea*
>
> *you pick the sugar*
> *and the pig picks—*

what—
hell? or is it

already heaven?
every choice a separation—

so it's back to square one, is it?
greensward and

river, elm and
appletree, now and the first

naming,
        no, not there

(the clink of Stein against
California: *there is no*

       there
       there)—

you need a way
onward, out of the

pippin emptiness
of definition—

you were not born here?
elsewhere:
and growing up elsewhere made elsewhere seem natural—
even the train tracks on Arbutus Street
wailed otherworlds and distance into the night

so did you foresee now?
no:
forward, in those other days, printed an elongated line, un-
interrupted into seed and curiosity:
but whoever branches on the angular
begins to feed on leavings

so when did the preachers start to plant magnolias
on Larch Street?

a path through bush is not possible unless
singing invents one:

> or dreams do, those that
> drum the edges of settled territory,

strike the way that rainbows slide ahead, re-
verberating—

> think rainbows in the dry country: think
> rain—

a path through forest is
contradictory:

> timber-stands deny mere
> wanderers,

devil's club and deadfall intruding, space con-
stricting, eye-dark and adderbright: moss hanging

> cirrus, air to earth, foliage
> drenched, stirring up cyclones—

a path through jungle means
street-savvy, knowing

> how to see around
> corners, where machetes cut

recognition, when to cross and when to
run: trafficking powderburns and clutching

air as white as tungsten, hot as tongues
kissing—

a path in the wood paints
safety: Robin Hood and Red's Woodsman playing

garden gnomes and bluebells and
let's pretend: no boa slithers silently through

yellow canary leaves, no lynx purrs
ledge-high hunger, no danger lurks *here,* say the

expurgated storybooks:
touch wood—

how the mind runs unknowingly: say
    hickory, and three mice tick

        up and down the clock as though
        no time had rung by:

say *Mary* and the garden breaks out in
    rowed maids and

        cockleshells—but what if you
        tried to stay:

would the blind mice tarry,
    or all of a sudden

        run widdershins
        after the cat in the lonesome room—

the bell boy, too, would he pawn his horn?
    the black sheep steal away with Jill?

        (so easily the goose words
        trip into serial:*watch this space:*

maybe Mary just wanted
    rumple in her life instead of

        Euclid's schoolhouse and
        dickering with Blue)—

you merely know that a hickory's standing
    down by the water, still,

that clothes hang checkered on the
lowest limb,

and yes, for sure, someone older,
ungulate and pruned,

is bound to be talking-to:
don't go near—

can anyone say *rowan* without
martin any more,

the Laugh-in doors exploding into
repartee (memory twining

back, rose-hipped, to a
tv time when

laughter flattened the literalmen, Forrest
Gump had not yet neutralized the

Rowntree box, and
Garland sang):

now the rigid occupy the Pale House,
and doors are closed:

though every fall the swallows leave on
Martinmas, their tails forked in flight, and

rowan trees erupt
in poppy-throated berries:

does anyone understand the irony
of vivid ash and strangled tongue—

(apple pie, curd pie,
coconut, cherry,

rhubarb, rhubarb,
raisin-rasp berry—

listen:
9-year-olds

singing the schoolyard,
skipping double-dutch and

happy, till O-U-T *spells*
out-you-must-go:

they're learning
borders as they grow,

the power of leaving out
as well as the covert

subtleties of
taking turns)—

Adam under the oak tree
felt the acorn fall

    and blamed Eve, naming
    each seed in curses:

Odysseus
ordered the tree cut down,

    tied himself to it,
    stabbed the bole in the eye:

Bligh, cast adrift, planned
a half-timbered revenge: Banks

    gathered as much,
    chucked the acorns overboard,

insisting hearts of oak could float and
history would cross the tropics sturdily in

    undisputed rows:
    the hills were levelled:

others reminisced:
but gravity had been discovered—

they tell stories
(surprised again by

unfamiliarity)
of Copper Inuit afraid of trees:

not the trees themselves,
enclosure,

the crack of branches
barracking

like ravens you can't predict
and cannot see:

lynx shadow,
black-robed ghosts muttering

pax, pax, and touching
te absolve to themselves

as though:
as though *sound*

made sense
bracketed

by things and not
telling:

they tell silence
as though narrative

did not exist
there: loss and

blueberry picking,
plain—

the Viking encyclopedia does not help
when you look for more about the *nim* tree:

> Nîmes is there, trading in fruit and wine
> from Roman times, and five-star Nimitz
>
> admiring the fleet, Nimrod the hunter, that's
> you perhaps, horn in hand, ears
>
> cocked for the knights who cry *nee*—
> (the wall of reference books collapses
>
> under the weight of excess—*nimiety*:
> 'too much' of course:
>
> the curious cat having to dance away
> from satisfaction):

the old sailors knew a thing or two,
turnips in the hold and nimbus on the far horizon:

you have to go to find out, no matter what,
n'importe, actually seek

India and all its distance, the air carrying
sandalwood and *nim*, heat and rain—

go, look at the old books:
always a man with a double-bitted axe

hurls his arms at hardwood,
horses haul stubborn stumps into

what might yet become a field, a bonfire rants
lithographs of hell into a night sky, and

two suspendered men in check shirts draw a
crosscut saw through an

old-growth fir:
they pause only for

pen-and-pencil visitors to gape at
magnitude, theirs, the trunk's, and be awed—

later, unsure,
these waist-coated callers will write of

raw, thrilling, dark, uncivil, savage, endless and
(there: they'll use the

London pages of the *Illustrated* to push away the
ardent adjectives they can't suppress, their

adverbs of desire, projecting fear *Over
There)*—

distance:
it's what the books appropriate, progeny and

power, *prospect* cut through time—
and how they'd have you read,

by ice and evil, paradise's lumberyard and
numbered sins—

although the sugar maples spell out
other ways to live,

the ordinary firs
a love affair with rain—

you know the history, then, the
person of this place?
Old Tom, you mean,
who said he hunted pheasants as a boy
where the house now stands,
the plot at the alley corner
where nothing grew but glass shards and coal,
the stranger who walked by
and asked for a chip of wood when the dying
spruce was felled, saying
'my grandmother planted that tree: I remember'

and what do you remember?
elsewhere,
suddenly St. George Street, the sword ferns and alderbush,
the wolfpack contests at St. George's Hall, riding the
wilderness of prurience,
the distances of learning love

is it enough to plant raspberries now in place of anthracite,
let pumpkins spill across the margin, onto the grass,
to write this Kitsilano into time?
May, the scent of lilac:
a slow breeze is drifting through the windowscreen

what does it mean
that a dog is barking
several houses down?

back again: a froth of salmon-pink
tips sumac into spring: tomorrow

scarlet
and in the meantime summer—

      freeze-frame the white cat
      twisting to lick a shoulder,

      sprats in a tad pool, yellow
      SLOW signs still cricking to last night's breeze

(the schoolyard chitters next to the walk
where a black mercedes draws up at 3,

old women's canes clatter
slowly over the judder bars)

      and keep the negatives:
      they will remind you,

      in the underbrush,
      of when you learned to read—

for F

(willow birch maple Scotch
pine: the children's trees, the

penny-whistle magic your
father could summon out of

emptylot scrub: the unsailable canoe
some parent's now anonymous

friend sent from away as a handsewn
souvenir: branches where

bare scraped legs hauled gravity
upsidedown and owls looked out on

olderthan: and Christmas, the
scent of it, peat bog and

bauble, the dog racing mud-high and
happy)—

Miss Bucknell, Miss Fox, in
elementary school explained that

silkworms fed on mulberry leaves:
a simple truth:

and you can't escape the
first things you learn: *wash your hands,*

tie your shoes,
turn out the light when the air raid siren whines—

(bywords:
although they paled beside the

unimagined origins of willow china-blue, Thai
fire-silk thread,

new narratives of
distance and surprise, taken in and

held
              like the

first lick of birthday cake at seven,
marbled and sweet)—

        Aesop's grapes came later,
        the boy who cried sassafras

        mixed up with
        broncoed matinees and

lamb's tails,
fields of enterprise you

never knew enough to plan for,
and saying sorry:

but over there in the mulberry trees,
buckled-up grade twos

still spin stories into silk,
wash their hands and say *excuse me*—

plating themselves in
pattern: they're not aware yet

they're learning already to say goodbye,
curfew tolling—

when you live with
plain pine, even the

names of elsewhere
take you travelling:

coffee, katsura,
Virginia live oak—

live:
think of how the trees

shade the dead, those we tack away
in brick and board and plaid blanket,

and those with us,
packages in fire and dust:

suppose it is the cones that think,
root and bark and clustered

needle
rearranging the world, to live:

the world no longer plain then,
nor only ours

(elsewhere *Menzies,*
Engelmann,

reverberate like *Bougainville,*
scrub pulses, resonates like *Amazon*:

the names we give to *them*
are names we use, looking out,

to look in, ourselves the object: who
else can know the subjectivity of pollen?)—

yes, those of you from the Temperate Zone
expect trees to flower: lilac, laburnum,

      Golgotha dogwood,
      even the pastel candlesticks of

horse chestnuts soon green,
telling the stories you ask of them,

      weeping memory and crossed future,
      bloom and blow:

but they don't ever train you for tropic, croton,
flamboyante intensities and bougainvillea, those

      nooks of red hibiscus trumpeting
      flesh and spent passion:

(the thin lips of may-white insist on
labour, penance, thorn,

      refuse the likelihood of ease: march
      protest before season)—

Bharati writes: *Tara Lata is five years old and headed
deep into the forest to marry a tree*—

transpires the folk story's family history, told by one
at the end of the line, scarcely breathing:

well, grandfathers die, uncles come and go, empires
end—perhaps the bride is *radiant*

and keeps her name, blood running through it,
hunting horns *ta-ra* glinting

rifles in the spinney, Atlanta burning, Ireland goodbye
(*pretty maids all in a row*)—

there is another possibility: she's wed the baobab,
the saurian shape that thunder takes

in the rain: maybe she's wrapped her arms
in epiphytes around its branches,

feeds on air and aspiration, dreams serpentine,
watches as her footprints walk away—

walking the boulevard,
do you ever touch the earth,
taste the cut of grass blades,
sing yourself (aye) in conifers and Kitsilano?
you tell your story travelling, trailing
others, those who live, and those who have lived, re-locating:
some were here before you, thinking themselves in place,
some will come after,
bones and bones, an underwood of dreaming

but can you say the near words yet?
catch and casement,
latched admission,
I and I, and I

cedar. the weaving of it. not the
single tree on a

white field. but density and wet
coast, cape and blanket, fronds

lacing
rain-shelter. totem.

cedar breathing. cedar
speaking.   bent box, fragrance.

traveller, dreaming
home—

great-uncle Thomas figures in
family annals

only because he was killed
felling a tree: more

must be known, but like cousin-
Hattie-who-was-killed-by-lightning

he filled a need because of
how he died:

somehow it's sacrificial,
each generation naming

one of its own to go,
as though the going gave the rest of them

security:
            against what?

            cloud-leopards in the trees,
            and firethorn?

no: only the grey river they've
built their house upon,

the air they take in and hold,
vanishing,

the innocence,
evaporation—

what you see if you face the moment square
is Tarzan swinging

heavy through the backlot
not airily through jungle trees

(making those games of *Let's pretend*—
ropes and branches, gradeschool acro-

batics—dangerous training):
all the ululation in the world

can't guarantee the gymnast won't
slip off the balance beam,

the planted sapling grow: or maybe that was
always the burrowing intention,

the slick film on the surface of war years,
nudging towards emptiness

(those old stories all invented
rabbit holes and toad hollows—

even Kipling knew that tigers could rip the
jugular, the Snow Queen

freeze)—but you didn't have to know then you
couldn't fly:

remember that cape? the confident rash steps
along the makeshift clothesline?

you can't circle back to such faith,
the first tree's already cut

(the one you were heading to,
once: officials called it rotten

years ago)—
now the enemies are digitized, fire's

tripped, even the reel's been cast aside:
and as soon as the stories forge ahead

guy-wires disappear
against the blue screen—

at the stud farm outside
Budapest, for instance,

four men in uniform re-enact
the last battle against the Turks—

they've trained their stallions to
lie low in hollows,

not flinch at the
bullet crack of the whip above their ears:

lie somnolent,
in hiding,

till at command they rise
already set for dust and instant war—

      pandemonium:
      applause—

but the men have put away
the old swords,

brandish only frown now and
plum vodka,

for tourists:
a locust blooms purple by the

souvenir shop, the rail fence is
painted tidy—

    mind you, the border's
    close: and poppies there

    storm arteries
    through the lunging hills—

or look for St. Denys, the patron of Paris: you find the
island in the Seine where he 'preached with great

success'—and so anticipate the scent of fresh baguette
wafting across the parc, *tilleul* and camomile—

instead you meet 'Rusticus-a-priest who was
beheaded with him,' and stop, breathless:

who was the axeman, you wonder:
what great offence sent him down the road,

ached him into duty and maybe regret?
did he go drinking after, empty a flask in the

ivy wood with a pack of rowdies, random and grey?
or with chapped lips mutter rosaries into safety,

turn Denys into Dionysius-the-Unknower, make
history out of murk and yeast and desiccant mistake?

take the i away: maybe it's loss he wants:
Dionysus he looks for, not the other: *god of trees*

in the headless, sensing night, moths and dancing:
maybe the 10-year-old he used to be, boy-on-the-farm, still

wanders there in the dark, awkwardly tilling,
stooking hay, learning to sharpen scythes at the

dampened whetting stone,
before he took orders, I mean—

drunk:
like starlings at a mountain ash, over-

come by opportunity,
stubbies in a clutch and the cohort daring: un-

anchored,
and not the time anyway to call *uncle*:

you catch the hunger only later, the
backwards mirror

laughing at
wretchedness and stubborn pride:

the taste of burnt cork still
sad on the tongue,

conkers,
early morning—

the traveller's tree,
says the guidebook to Madagascar,

collects a pint of drinking water
in the pocket where each frond joins the main stem:

> in the photograph,
> long leaves fan upward, call you into

> late afternoon,
> and there you are in the picture, trekking

> thirstily, next to the sea,
> across some plain, around a

> jungled mountainside:
> > macaques scatter fractious at the

> > celluloid
> > loop of your caravan

(so little you know—
do you ask yourself *where does this*

drinking water come from? why are you
thirsty in the rain?)—

> your mind's desert fills with
> sand and bones, O'Keeffe

> among the Joshua trees,
> saguaro bent on a burning horizon:

the cup is coating as you watch it dry,
dusty with film—

what else do you see?
November, fire, February rain,
eyes looking back, out of the laurel hedge,
electric fences, cold avoidance, old magnolia

at least those old movies told it straight:
good guy or bad, get yourself caught by the

wrong gang, posse, revolutionary mob or
plain fate and you'll swing from branch or

rafter—*Hanged by mistake* says one
Tombstone tombstone—

though sometimes the good guys would
side-track the wicked world, and

save the hanging for later (you learned early
that honesty caused a stir)—

>the parachutes, though,
>caught in the trees,

>hint at something else,
>the air men scrambling to

>undo themselves before
>cuts or cold or an enemy

>sniper gets them first, the untold in-
>dignity of tangle:

maybe they knew that other story,
the one that never showed at the matinee,

real life happening
off stage, in the shade of a black elm, or

at the back of a gabled house on a
blind curve of cul-de-sac, or

over there in the papered room, where
ordinary people live—

the coffee shop in the mountain logging town
doubles as post office and book supply:

magazines are racked along the west wall:
Tongue, Flesh, Score, Swank, Stun: the girl

ignores them,
wipes a table down with cheesecloth,

once, fold, pause, another swipe and
done:

in front, the girl? her mother?
someone's placed *Birds, Blooms, Wrestling*, and

Rav 4, and lower down
People, Cosmo, Spiderman:

                  the wildflowers on the vinyl tabletop are
                  real: a bent-backed man in a grey shirt

                  licks a stamp and presses his envelope
                  twice before the girl takes it:

                  a bell rings when he lumbers out,
                  pitches across to the lodge:

Handgunner, Quilting:
                  one truck rumbles by, shakes the windows:

Maximum PC is last month's issue, and
dog-eared: the girl

turns away from the door, refills the coffee pot:
noon—

while under the dragon tree
     (the guidebook says in Tenerife),

the Guanche once dispersed justice,
     the tree's red resin a sign of blood,

     or maybe health (they cannot say,
     they've disappeared,

     into myth and travel books,
     empire's parenthesis—

     the Mac-Paps, too, are dying, or
     already gone)—

but *Drago* survives: *dracaena draco:*
     drago milenario,

     icon, remnant from before
     the advancing ice—

on the feast day of the Immaculate Conception, three priests and
two rows of hard-eyed women trail effigies through the lime-
washed streets of La Laguna, candles in hand, blue penitence and
racing rosaries:

around the corner Harry Potter toughs it out with Frodo and the
night (it is December 2002, politicians stiffen into attitude, the
Lonely Planet speaks of accommodation):

so where are the saints and streetcar drivers?
    railing into stone:

on frieze and bronze horse, even George is
    distant, riding rigid and sure the

        corridors of Aragon, the parliaments and naves
        of a different far away and long ago,

        though now in the north a slick and
        separate danger threatens from the sea:

fresh volunteers, their world stained with power, have left today
with bare hands to join the mending line along the oil-soaked
Galician shore, chanting *Nunca maís*, angry, the fires are
burning—

be wary of Teide, volcano:
    it is the island's heart

(do not be fooled by the subtropic snow,
    the empty Guanche caves,

        the poster wars and postcard racks and
        incandescent movie-house marquees):

        the dragon stirs, intent on
        holding the island,

        bristles its leatherback leaves,
        fielding time—

you say you envy trees their rootedness,
their green stability: and when, like

yellow tamarack, they drop their needles,
you say *compost*, and find

more ways to wish yourself still,
branches the wind blows through,

new buds the colour of
old family, and

no one calls you wrong:
            but you are:

the forest travels,
slips at night down to the skinny pool and

drinks stars,
romps at the edge of prairie

till cypress hills rise
and tumble—

Birnam, Birnam, the trees murmur,
mouthing their password to walking—

you ought to know this:
roots do not fix you, do not give you

precedence
or granite the right to endure:

let the wind take you riding as it does them:
give yourself rainbows:

for maybe they're stops on a streetcar route
    you haven't taken yet,

way points on a wet trip home, swaying:
    kukui, cashew, loblolly bay,

      tamarisk, calabash, kapok: imagine
the capped conductor singing out the names—

      litchi, loquat, kumquat, tung—
his words flapping the bleared glass as the

budcar slips along the rails, ripping
    riverbends:

passengers are ringing
    here and next and here and next to

disembark, wrestling
    backpacks, pelted hats,

      garden-variety bumbershoots
down the metal steps:

where do they go, those
    rainclad strangers? along

      cinnamon street or *nutmeg,* maybe,
into the dry country,

petrified,
    as far away as they can from the

      one or two who want to stay on, to the
roundabout they say you'll find at the end of the maybe line—

think monkey-puzzle, think
getting off the—*ow*—ground,

grabbing *on* and bloodied, zero
besides: art earthbound, *eh?*

the heart of it, what the *ear*
hears, argon and air, even

i, i, and *i,* o.d.,
bone, and lost victory:

you live the edges, rasp and
bristlecone—pining

for a centre you don't believe in,
pinnacle and being: being something,

nothing, twisted branches on the
same *i.v.*—take your dreams

to the nearest emergency room: they'll
scour you out: think monkey

puzzle, broken sleep, letterpress and
seizing—

so in a Kitsilano garden, then,
you hear the world conversing,

     writing I in winter,
     underwood in time:

finches in the sleet-bare japonica
rap, prattle purple gossip, chatter

     play-ground swings, the flap of
     my toy, mine—

quince, quince, the gall of it: voicebox
scrapping at *they never,*

     didn't they? they didn't—or *they did*—or
     just behave: a flit and then

already gone, the
sigh of silence empty then a

     breath, then a
     breath, then an

       afternoon
       snow:

in Rajasthan the orange-sareed women
plant trees against the desert,

> grey-green acacia, the parch igniting
> god in agapanthus leaves—

on the farm in Manitoba, the old
grandfather's grandfather planted

> a wind-break first, poplar bluff
> against the north, and winterthorn—

rosemary grows now
on roadbanks in the Manawatu,

> olives in Andalucía, everywhere
> a line before the dust, against clay—

the grass is terrifying, the old man says,
    electric green, each blade

vibrating into the eye—
    it's one of the rare moments now

he stumbles into meaning:
    most days he lives

in a tree house of the mind, chattering
    up-in-the-air adjectives and

out-of-pocket nouns, and says
    I mean it, though

only gentle guesses
    can take apart the code: *I need*

pilgrims to hold up the roof,
    he says.

he's pleased when you
flick on the ceiling light:

you've become a torch bearer
wherever it is he

camps in the long overnight,
and you climb, climb, as

fast as you can when he
lets down a ladder of metaphor,

carefully lifting your feet
from the terrifying green—

87

in the room upstairs, in Harlech on the sea,
in the pub across from the castle entrance

(*4-and-6* when it opens at 8),
you hear the men below singing

Ar Hyd y Nos and *The Ash Grove*
over a pint or three: the voices

cling at the edge of coal and custom—
clattering glasses track the publican, *Time*

gentlemen please, and rumbled laughter
echoes into the walls—you wait:

no fletchers show at the turrets, no
weavers in the woolsheds, no

giants loom at the casement window:
the hills are bare . . .
                              all long the night—

up a tree,
pining, *o-*

pining:
oh—

who do you talk with over the garden hedge?
writers, rakers, reachers, ghosts:
husbandmen and harrowers,
planters of apple trees,
attending careful silences the way that
caragana boys trade hockey cards and the facts of life

and now?
tilling the border,
exchanging seedlings, marigolds,
talismans against departing

and you enumerate these moments?
yes:
no: they simply are, and happen,
ring growing ring,
like love, in generation,
grandchild on a waterslide, laughing summer back
from the vanishing

so what do you count as neighbourhood?

the poet sits at the Underwood, tapping out
two-fingered tomes in daily measures:

the grammar immaculate, the typos
triple-X'd, the nip of scotch beside him

a promise, for after: each day
he writes to find imaginary space,

but *after* eludes him: always
he tangles the keys, loses himself

in roots and origins, *before*
calling him back, vermiculate,

to leaf mould, decay, dogwood in the
autumn, cruciform:

even when he rests he plunders
history, until distilling wears him

thin, and calculation
cases the vernacular in ice—

(*bark is worse than* . . . there's that
    cliché again—better lasso it

    while you can [*trite*, past part.
    terere, to rub, meaning *too much*

    rubbed—frayed, not erased—like
    temper, tongue, time, intemperate and

    longing]: tied, hanging on until the rope
bites)—

give over—
you do not need to be here,

the masters tell you
that only *absenting*

promises enlightenment: *detach*—
sit under the BO tree—you must

dispossess yourself
to find the ONE:

>   *but look, there: already*
>   *you're counting the beautiful—*
>
>   *naming your lover, who beckons you*
>   *with bread and a cup of*
>
>   *unclouded water, brings you*
>   *salt kisses, fingers touching*
>
>   *the small of the back, spun*
>   *river music, silk, crimson, here,*
>
>   *the vagrancy of pale gardenias,*
>   *and, yes, time—*

93

BODHI:
disconnect:

    no:
    the apple

    turned us away from separation—
    now every one of the senses

    draws us back, into
    beautiful (the present tense of

    sorrow) and
    being here,

    tree—

and yet why type except to write yourself
elsewhere, *into* the underwood: take the

beeline, the el, track the A-train,
all will get you near,

the woodwinds' moody blue, the
red jet of alphabet and horn—

go ahead, whistle 3, 2, 1: you're carried
quick as commas past the full stop,

over the puzzling wall,
across whatever divides, paralysis, ravine—

but will you then be able to utter *I*,
I (without halting) *love?*—

when will *there* become *here*, you-and-I,
alongside the branch water,

limbs tangling in trumpet flowers,
spelling the world in ease and green desire:

o, ours, the moment
travelling (not exacting instruments and *why*),

stroking—
out of asterisk & into ampersand,

out of character & into stutter, out of
stet, out of *stet*, into syllable—

think of the red trees, what they say,
the leaves just off the round, or

edge-milled,
penny for your thought

      (smoke and copper beech,
      clustered and grim:

      battlefield and gunnery practice,
      sticks and stones)—

they place coins on the eyes of the dead,
to help the bloodless pay the ferryman—

the weight could
drown them—

      but think of sumac in the fall,
      scrappy as jazz in a Big Easy funeral,

      saying what *is*, nothing more,
      foil and flare—

from above, the forest looks a canopy of birds, leaves
folded into lorikeets, green wings & tulips, scarlet &

jarring: underbranch, the high flyer's blind—grevilleas
squawk rainbows, parrots skein tree to tree &

green snakes curl in supposition: yes,
suppose you're the flyer, bodiless & bland, aimless as

cottonwood seed (why do you say *suppose*?) floating
into a different hemisphere: your brain says

latitude and reads it twice, underhanded—*bipolar*?
(categories of the mind: *resist*): in dissent

is laughter, kookaburras raiding the light & chasing
texture into the airwaves—*simplification, 1 plus 1:*

plus 1?: no, the bare complexities of mimicry
defy knowing true, or knowing only

one face of true (the look of leaves, say,
the minimum of green)—

the tracery of veins beats otherwise, bleeding
tulips into the upside-down, and unpinning wings—

for the farmer, the first surprise was finding
artifacts with the plough, metal heads

piercing the red earth's surface with
aquiline noses, grinning mouths, protruding eyes:

the second involved the archeologists,
the careful pits they dug in his field, changing

history and harvest and Chengdu—
now they call this place Sanxingdui, the mount of

three stars, and now it's occupied by
their imaginations:

> the unnamed, undiscovered people who
> lived there so many centuries ago

> (35, 36, under the mountain)
> give up their toss of

> remnant bronze and elephant tusks
> without disclosing meaning—

even the archeologists are surprised:
they count the separate pieces,

sort them into cabinets and cages, see
vermilion and think *sacrifice*,

ritual blood and knives—
> but you think *discard*:

a new emperor clearing away old
fragmentary signs of power, a new

priest, silencing the icons of a
late persistent faith:

all you understand
is that you still seek understanding,

so fasten on what they also found there:
bronze trees, brittle and hidden, underground—

you put them back together,
these trees,

they stand twelve feet tall,
each branch hangs with

jade disks and collared rings, and
clapper bells in peacock-dress, and

tiny birds with hooked beaks and human heads
and feathers marked in scalloped lines—

the archeologists
say they might be money trees: they know of

earthenware branches hanging rich with coins,
where human figures pluck talents as they would

peaches, where apes and elephants
clamber high towards the goddess of prosperity—

but no, it won't do: the gift at Sanxingdui
is not purchase

but the power of speaking:
the ancients called their first script

tree-language—
no-one can read it now

(but listen to the clapper bells
score the air, the metal birds sing

minims in their
underground forest):

syllables run where the plough has
turned them toward the stars—

finding the words:
that was the fourth surprise—

for LR

they root on alphabets, arbutus trees (*madrone*): no ploughed and
furrowed earth holds them, they feed on petroglyph and sandstone, lean

out over clifftops to sound the ocean, spell its chill appeal, inflect the light
that rises daily from the Gulf: they cluster where strawberry meadows

dissipate in underwood, salal, living on edges, pushing at the rules of
ordinary, peeling bark all summer like fan dancers at the red mill, teasing

meaning out of motion, playing *field*: no exhibitionist maple, these,
disrobing October—no, they savour consonance, glossing green, compose

angled metaphors of coast and coping: the giants grow slowly on these
islands, Gabriola, Valdes: they teach the written, lichened rock to read—

downsoft,
deceptive,

spindles of spiked impression,
how suddenly they're golden in the fall,

the tamarack's needles—

the first time you brush against them,
you fear resistance, the

prick of holly, spur of blue spruce,
defensive, arrogant, knowing:

and are undone—

the many names compound your green
uncertainties (hackmatack, *larix*, larch):

and how to read past this pseudonym disguise
except—here—touch tells all,

caressing:

everyone has a *once-upon-a-time*,
soft light and hesitation (*not yet not yet*),

identity slipping the body, dis-
appearing into

now:

what does it matter what you call it,
cotillion, cotyledon, cell division, love

(the green music of the tamarack or the
deep burning yellow)—

lean into this moment:

learn that *once* happens again,
hands hold fast as

age daunts and delays
(*unser*, the old word:

we two):

stops
are only temporary, straw fields for

spark to light in
(or angle-bracket pain:

accept both)—

you're living somewhere then that
winter cannot startle into thorn

or unreal emptiness: the tamarack invites,
tells you every day the continuities

of beauty naked and close:

yes, the needles fall:
years are deciduous—

surprise them into
waking,

dream the stories through—

who is the one, say, who planted the
first jesting sycamore

in the plots of land they signed over to
those who died of the plague, turned

London squares into tiny parks where
nannies roll up in uniform, old men

ogle, and furled barristers, each closing the
wrought-iron gate, cut

kiddy-corner past the
weathered benches and mottled bark—

someone's great-grandmother,
not more than a dozen generations back:

you can see her now,
bending,

hands in the earth by the green trunks,
tending fresh the dappled light,

and marigolds—

is this where you live, then, Kitsilano?
affirmation's not so easy: it is
not enough to say where the breath comes from,
oxygen exchange and carbon dioxide:
simply, the trees breathe,
and you—I—with them

so now you celebrate—
the neighbourhood that breathes you into place,
the space you wander in, imagine?
I imagine here, aye,
inhale, exhale
(in Inuktitut the People's word for breath
is also the word for poetry),
living is travelling,
rooted,
free

the grammar of grass, the syntax of
hemlock needles, indigo and interrupted

lexicons of motion
tumble you into another tongue:

is it you, the underwood,
huckleberry speaking back at the

hardscrabble stump ranch you call a farm
(you yourself you've distanced out of

earshot, into
fungus:

you in trunk and crossing branches,
fern, stem and capillary, tendrils

coupling,
promise and desire):

do you listen?
hear all the

other shapes of meaning? or
plough along in the

naming furrows, counting
rift,

dissecting
parataxis in the leaves—

in those other days,
you could sit on the lawn in the Bay of Islands,

G&T in hand, cricketers in white, croquet mallet
close by, and save for the lemon trees think it

Hampshire:
            lemon blossom, though—

remember Kyprios in spring, oranges in
Córdoba or Fez, polished days and topiaried nights?—

or think of Tai Tokerau, the Bay before it
was the Bay and

bowlers trimmed Kerikeri into
domain and

seedpods tipped it under
Capricorn—

breathe in—
            taste the fragrance

every way you can—citrus
            disarray—

fermenting now, the juniper berries in your glass
tumble you back through time to the

red pohutukawa trees, the rainbow ocean
breaking at the edge of where-The-People-live:

but you cannot stay there,
tarakihi in the food basket, the sun warm on

bare shoulders, the first canoes just singing
star-certain onto shore: you're

shawled in an afghan now, grousing away
in what the nurses call the nicer terrace,

though revelling still in the dislocating tonic,
sour-sweet—

romping through the *Funk & Wagnall's*
you find definition well-covered—

eucalypt for instance, fifty,
a hundred varieties? a kind of

myrtle they say, but that doesn't
take you far: *vaccinium*

(a blueberry, nothing to do with
cows): which eases you along

to *whortleberry*, dialectal
variant of *hurtleberry*

(= *huckleberry*, so they say,
not the red kind but the blue)

& *huckle* (= *hip*) trips you
headlong back to hurtle: some

huckster's probably behind
the roundabout, pitching eu-

calyptus oil at the fair
grounds, swinging promises

& barking, covering up
the scribbly truth, tail wagging

the dog &—what else?—
romping—

for RL

and after the cantering
      trail-ride,

the old bay gelding,
      hot and

unsaddled,
      rolls in the dust,

while under an
      overhang,

a young grey
      rubs his rump

against the pitchpine:
      afternoon

hovers,

mirages

haze the valley floor in
      sly reservoirs,

corral the air in
        spent hollows,

thunderless with
        waiting—

breathing:
        breathing in &

breathing
      in, catching the

scent of resin and
      dried dung—

whatever tomorrow brings,
      including

nothing,
      fireworks,

and more of the same, it's
      penned here,

taut,
      parched—

while somewhere else,
      pooled,

at the back of the eyes,
      grass fields

roll forever, and
      all the animals

are running,
      running—

don't think, just listen: the pear tree in the back
garden, springwhite and then swelling August,

bees humming silence into
quiet:

listen:
a Thursday afternoon carpenter hammers four nails in the

distance, the woman next door calls out to her children,
boys, who do or don't take notice,

yet, *dinner's nearly ready,*
a float plane drones overhead,

trundles into noise, reverberates,
strips the air like a single string of contrail:

suddenly
listen:

a bright red (how do you know?)
dump truck

rumbles along beside the boulevard, squeals
butterfly sharp at the corner octagon: and

four boys (two from next door?)
shriek into terrier-talk,

giddy with water balloons and sun: and suddenly
birds, birds, everybird and fifty,

flapping in the pear, the air a cloud of
chatter, abrupt and

(vanish):

stems and even leaves holding still, until
another go-cart rattles past,

green light,
another bee—

Narayan singing the deodar, Derek Walcott the
casuarina, each invents ways to touch the sky

(trunks the air can wind tendrils around,
spaces for rain to dance in): they write

roots like blackberries growing upside down, relating
where they stand (Malgudi, sure)

or how they travel to find *that place, here*
(or *this place, there*), St. Lucia questing:

where is the sky climbing to,
where does the rained earth ease away?—

and which of these old
stormwashed melodies does

Kitsilano sing, with the
border near and ice not far from summer:

salt wind & maple? (the foreshore daily
drafting custom, change itself the

currency of living): do not resist
the sky to come, the

variance of repetition, but neither
rush to preach entropy—

remember nearby,
the neighbourhood of trees:

in the maple scrub,
children again are building swings—

horsefeathers, goosefeathers, catkins, cream,
the suddenness of silliness, basswood, bream,

mulberry, nannyberry, elderberry, yew,
swing upon a sycamore: I will too—

they sound like country rock,
groups that junior high and a set of drums

assemble in the rec room: *Garry Oak & Holly;*
Cherry Jackpine; Pussy Willow Shag; or just

Buckeye—the attitude's key: shapes the image,
voice breaking later into sweet jam and surly—

>   it's not the looking back that hurts,
>   or looking forward: it's looking back

>   *at* the looking forward, knowing the
>   trees stripped bare, lost bark and expectation

>   burying desire: where is the strut now?
>   (cycling—into the woods)—

but what's that sound?
(an early morning treble sax,

struggling into the lower notes,
and pitch)—

all curly hair and loose limbs, you pant a rough trail
past Sibelius and early tiger lilies into the

white Karelian woods: two women are laughing
in a sauna nearby, the voices carry:

you tell yourself *brisk,* knowing lingonberry
bushes are pushing into bud, the birchbark's

bright and peeling, the women laughing, steam
rising where the damp earth kicks into the sun:

you think of birch twigs stirring the stone kettle,
lakewater lapping cold at the rock border, growl

times tables, clamber into granite—the women
running to the water, linking arms at the

elbows and
laughing—

reading by fragments, Thomas Wharton's
Salamander, for instance: *One carries one's*

upbringing, she said. Even into the forest,
the inky dark where you or anyone uncovers

dragons—(not monsters, aberration-coloured,
bracketed and read:

Wharton resets the world the colour of
telling, well-deep and road-long): take that

porcelain way through China, *the*
Dragon-Vein Stretching a Thousand Miles:

it's riddled with everyperson's tale,
his, yours, the ferryman's,

they're all connected somehow, 'flowing like
dragon's blood under its hide'—

and this: the salamander, *the little dragon*
that dwells in fire without being consumed:

he's reassurance
for people who work with paper (writer,

printer, reader, typesetters all): *The book*
invents another book

(the reader knows this already,
hears the storyteller's passion, the promise a

blank page holds, the kenning
doubt, the bamboo silence that ripples twice

just before it breaks into letterpress and castle)—
listen:

whatever you discover
you can read again,

lance and dragon, blood and bone, tortoise
onionskin and opportunity:

the minutes that spell you into
maybe yet

will bring you if you want them to
seven oceans past the forest's edge,

the lips' parentheses, into
unknowing, fire—

what is it the children ask from the rumble seat?
are we there yet—

and what do you answer?
nearly, almost, soon

is it the truth?
truth is the gap we live
alongside then and next, delay and expectation,
spaces we make by speaking,
clearings the forest invents: silence, storybooks,
disruption

are you here yet?

swanning round Paris,
cassis and lindenbloom till

past midnight and then
pernod, night and day

crooning, sky dissolving:
floating undersmoke

and thunder sailing,
seine becomes starshine—

a letter in the *Times-Picayune*
complains of palm trees:

the hundreds of long fronds
live for a year before they wither and fall

and must be broken to disposable size,
pigeons live in the upper branches,

cracked eggs and dead squabs
litter the ground below:

it is a sermon—

another letter states that hell is
real and here but isn't worth mentioning,

having just mentioned it—

hell is perhaps an endless row of
palm trees,

the groundskeeper on holiday—
or else that's heaven,

depending on what you think about
heaven: is it there and neat,

or living here unruly?—

these needy letter writers picture
birth and death and

then imagine they'll be free of both,
apparently—

perhaps they do not notice
the wind touching leaves into cradles,

thunder breaking like
breath on the body,

the long eyelash of rain—

for LJP

he'd have laughed at the metaphor: *nurse log*—
not laughed exactly (not his style, guffaws)

but he savoured irony, the eyes more than the
corners of the mouth, tasting contradictions,

opportunities for play—*nurse log*: the mossy giant
whose bark feeds the generation after—huckleberries

shinnying sunlight, halfling cedar-fronds that
hardly wear yet the living they've already

won from the already gone, the treeness they've
inherited—

under furze eyebrows, his eyes would dance
at contrarieties, the voice low:

peace, he'd write,
just before his letters ended—

logging on:
you learn others by minutes, yourself

by degrees, in prototype and stereo,
the music of one sphere

(the one you recognize)
playing in the foreground

(the understory running
counterpoint,

minutiae taking hold and then the
keys opening elsewhere, opening

into elsewhere, ravens and rimu,
alphabets of the unfamiliar):

not what you name that matters
(*that* and *those* and *they*)

but what's shadowed in corners,
looking back between the branches in

energy and waving—

outside, each of us is
nearly seeing

(rambling about in energy and
waving):

at intervals, by syllable,
we stretch beyond the cobweb reach of

limitation,
step off at the ends of lines and

when we can
into underwood: the mind

easing between the
cardinals, lighting

there, discovering, and there, dis-
connecting,

each minute a fraction of desire:

ferryboat, tramline,
continental drift,

all carry us through
virtual time—

      eye and eye and
      eye—

and yet the single heart beats out its
own *meanwhile*:

spells away the expedition's axes,
geometry's co-ordinated planes, and

highrigger, faller,
journeyman scribe,

planting a traverse the long way here,
turns inward

      (where?)

into the forest:
      this far,

      so far,
      I am:

          here—

Acknowledgments

I am indebted to many others for the echoes here—composers, collectors, painters, and makers of film: Tom Thomson and Georgia O'Keeffe, Aesop and La Fontaine, Andersen, Anne Rice, Tolkien, Rowling, Burroughs, Baum, and the Brothers Grimm— and to songbooks, garden books, travel guides, the *Oxford Book of Saints*, and scores of others. The powerful voices of contemporary writers—among them those of Thea Astley, Bharati Mukherjee, R.K. Narayan, Timothy Taylor, Derek Walcott, Thomas Wharton, and Judith Wright—inform several sections of this poem. Especially I wish to acknowledge Chief Khatsahlano of the Squamish band, and his grandson, the Sun'ahk elder August Jack Khatsahlano (c.1876-1967), whose name lives on in a Vancouver neighbourhood.

With thanks (again) to Laurie and Jack and Ron, who keep asking me to hear, and to Hiro and Jay as well, for listening—

About the Author

W.H. New grew up in Vancouver. A teacher, editor, essayist and constant traveller, he is the author of several commentaries on space, place and borderlands, and on short stories, language and literary history. In 2004 he was awarded the Governor General's International Award for Canadian Studies and the Lorne Pierce Medal for his contributions to critical and creative writing. *Underwood Log* is his sixth book of poetry.